Contents

Punchouts

Name _____

What Happened?

 The picture shows what happens at the beginning of *My Best Friend.* **Draw a picture of something that happens in the middle of the story. Then draw what happens at the end.**

Name _____

My Own Best Friend

 Draw a picture of you and your best friend doing something you love to do together.

Name _____

Alphabet Review

Andy Apple

Benny Bear

Callie Cat

 Penmanship Practice

A A   a a

B B   b b

C C   c c

Begins with Bb or Cc

Phonics Circle each picture whose name begins like the Alphafriend's name.

Word Play Name the picture. Print the letter that begins the picture name.

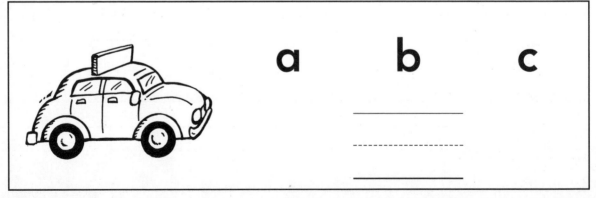

a   b   c

_____

- - - - - - -

_____

Name _____

Alphabet Review

Dudley Duck

Edna Elephant

 Penmanship Practice

D D   d d

E E   e e

Name _____

The Letters Dd and Ee

✏️ **Phonics** Draw a line from the Dd to pictures whose names begin with that letter sound.

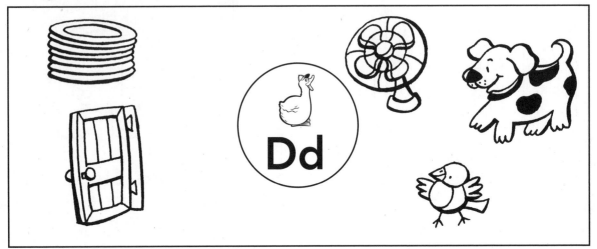

✏️ **Draw a line from the E to the matching letters.**

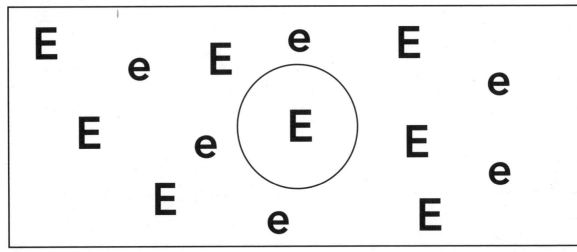

✏️ **Word Play** Name the picture. Print the letter that begins the picture name.

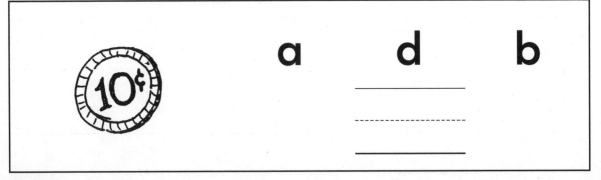

a   d   b

Name _____

Alphabet Review

Fifi Fish

Gertie Goose

Hattie Horse

 **Penmanship Practice**

F F   f f

G G    g g

H H   h h

Name _____

Begins with Ff, Gg, or Hh

Phonics Circle each picture whose name begins like the Alphafriend's name.

Word Play Name the picture. Print the letter that begins the picture name.

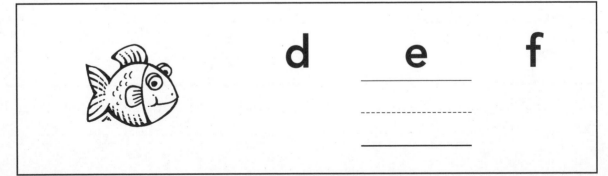

d   e   f

Name _____

Alphabet Review

Iggy Iguana

Jumping Jill

Penmanship Practice

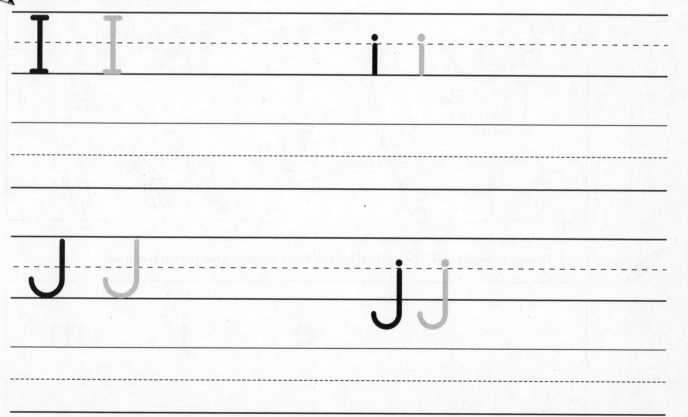

Name _____

The Letters Ii and Jj

Phonics Draw a line from the i to the matching letters.

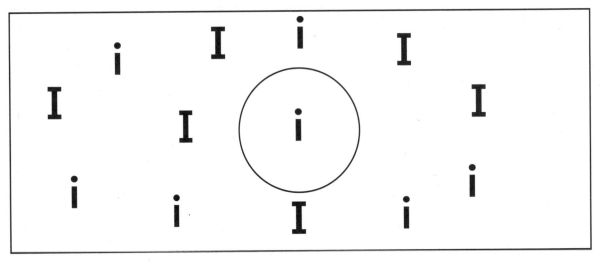

Draw a line from the Jj to the pictures whose names begin with that letter sound.

Word Play Name the picture. Print the letter that begins the picture name.

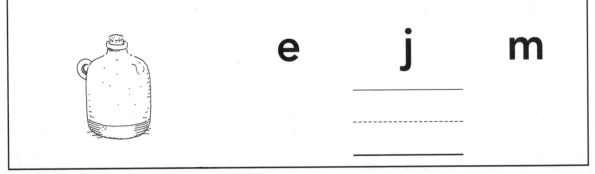

e   j   m

Name _____

Alphabet Review

Keely Kangaroo

Larry Lion

Mimi Mouse

Penmanship Practice

K K   k k

L L   l l

M M   m m

Name _____

Begins with Kk, Ll, or Mm

Phonics Circle each picture whose name begins like the Alphafriend's name.

Word Play Name the picture. Print the letter that begins the picture name.

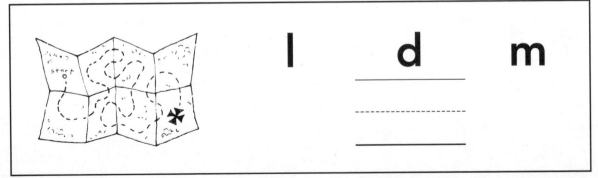

l   d   m

_____

Name ___Ben_____

Alphabet Review

Nyle Noodle

Ozzie Octopus

Pippa Pig

Penmanship Practice

Name _____

Begins with Nn or Pp

Phonics Circle each picture whose name begins like the Alphafriend's name.

Word Play Name the picture. Print the letter that begins the picture name.

g   _____   e   p

Name _____

Alphabet Review

Queenie Queen

Reggie Rooster

Sammy Seal

Penmanship Practice

Name _____

Begins with Qq, Rr, or Ss

Phonics Circle each picture whose name begins like the Alphafriend's name.

Word Play Name the picture. Print the letter that begins the picture name.

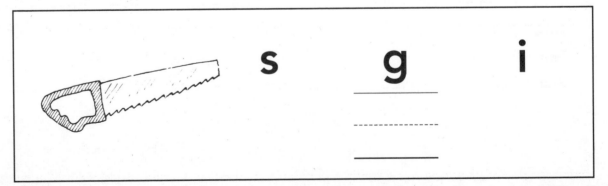

s   g   i

Name _____

Alphabet Review

Tiggy Tiger

Umbie Umbrella

Vinny Volcano

 Penmanship Practice

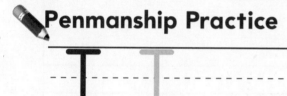

Name _____

Begins with Tt or Vv

Phonics Circle each picture whose name begins like the Alphafriend's name.

Word Play Name the picture. Print the letter that begins the picture name.

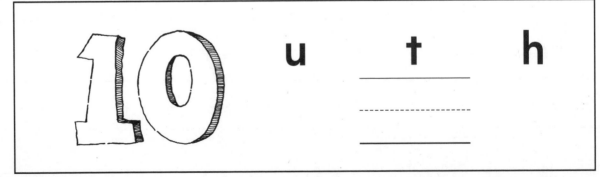

Name _____

Alphabet Review

Willy Worm

Mr. X-Ray

Penmanship Practice

W W   w w

X X   x x

Name _____

The Sounds for Ww and Xx

Phonics Draw a line from the Ww to the pictures whose names begin with that letter sound.

Draw a line from the Xx to the pictures whose names have the /ks/ sound.

Word Play Name the picture. Print the letter that begins the picture name.

f   w   o

Name _____

Alphabet Review

Yetta Yo-Yo

Zelda Zebra

✏ Penmanship Practice

Y Y

y y

Z Z

z z

Name _____

Begins with Yy or Zz

Phonics Draw a line from the Yy to pictures whose names begin with that letter sound.

Phonics Draw a line from the Zz to pictures whose names begin with that letter sound.

Word Play Name the picture. Print the letter that begins the picture name.

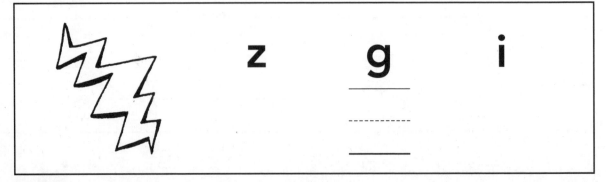

z   g   i

I See My

I

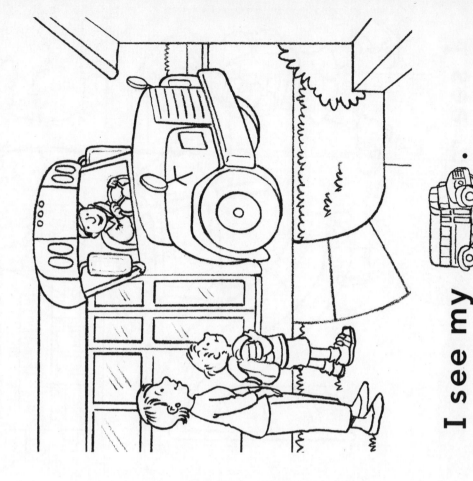

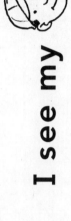

I see my  .

I see my  .

Back to School, Week 1, Day 3

I see my  .

I see my .

High-frequency words: *I, see, my*

I see my 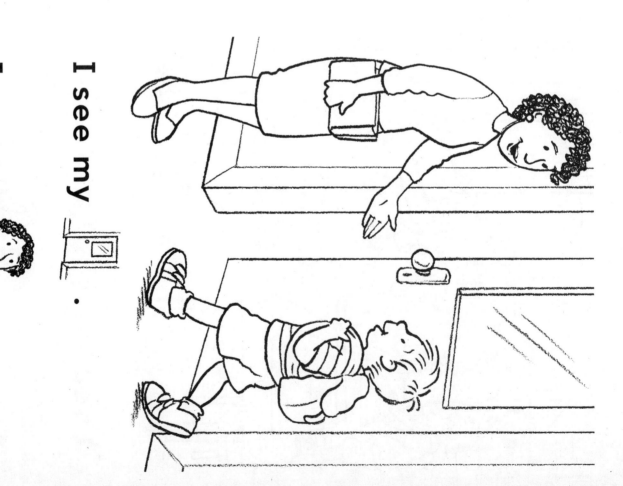 .

I see my .

I see my .

I see my .

I Like

I see a  .

I like 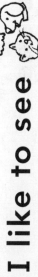 .

Back to School, Week 1, Day 5

I see  .

I like to see .

High-frequency words: *like, a, to*

I see a  .

I like  .

High-frequency words: *like, a, to*

I see a 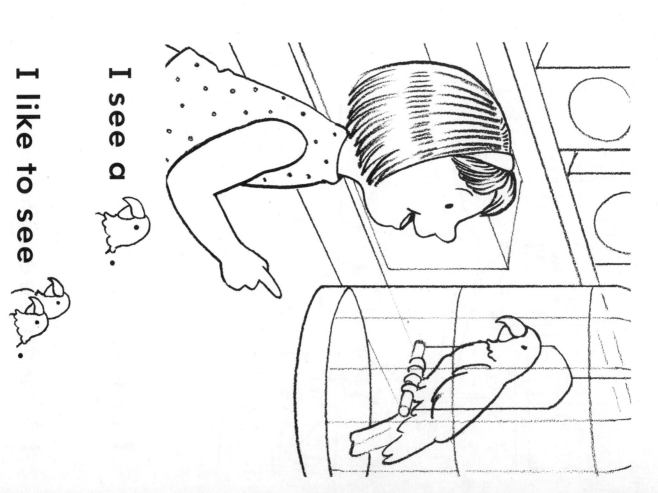 .

I like to see 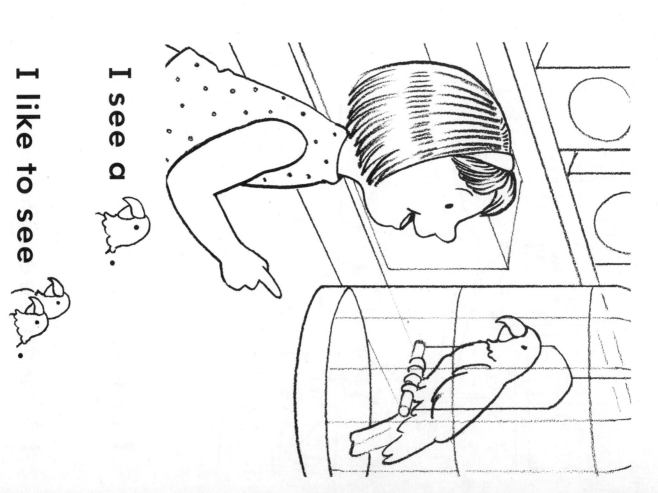 .

I Have

I have a  .

Here is my  for a 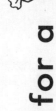 .

1

I have a 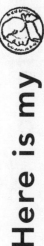 .

Here is a  for a .

4

High-frequency words: *here, for, have*

I have a  .

Here is my  for a .

High-frequency words: here, for, have

I have a  .

Here is my for a  .

Back to School, Week 2, Day 4

"Play!" Said the

"I play," said the .

"I play the ."

"Play!" said the .

"Play, play, play."

"I play," said the

"I play the  ."

"I play," said the

"I play the  ."

High-frequency words: *said, the, play*

The  Are Here

The  and the

go to a .

He and she see a .

Back to School, Week 3, Day 4

He and she see a .

The  are here.

High-frequency words: *she, are, he*

The  are here.

He and she like the  .

High-frequency words: *she, are, he*

The  are here.

He and she have  for the  .

Name _____

Begins with *m* or *s*

Think of each beginning sound. Write *m* or *s.*

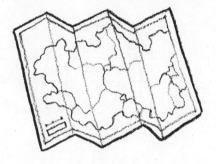

1. _____

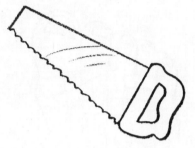

2. _____

3. _____

4. _____

5. _____

6. _____

7. _____

8. _____

9. _____

Theme 1: **All Together Now**   **35**

Name _____

Begins with *c* or *t*

Think of each beginning sound. Write *c* or *t*.

1. _____

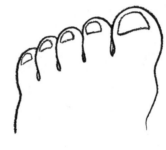

2. _____

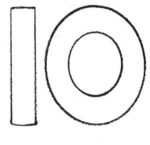

3. _____

4. _____

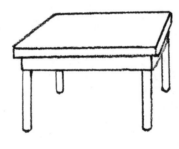

5. _____

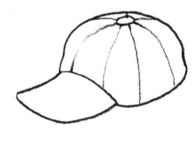

6. _____

7. _____

8. _____

9. _____

Name _____

Ends with *m*, *s*, or *t*

Think of each ending sound. Write *m*, *s*, or *t*.

1. _____

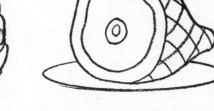

2. _____

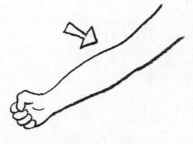

3. _____

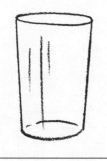

4. _____

5. _____

6. _____

7. _____

8. _____

9. _____

Theme 1: **All Together Now**   37

Name _____

Short *a*

Name each picture. Color the pictures whose names have the same vowel sound as  .

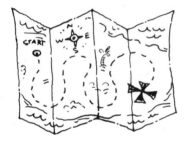

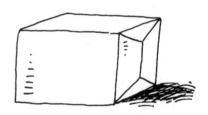

Name _____

Blending Short *a* Words

Blend the letter sounds. Then write the correct word for each picture.

c	a	t		h	a	t

1.

_____

2.

_____

Read the sentence. Circle the picture that goes with it.

3. Sam sat.

Theme 1: **All Together Now**   39

Name _____

Begins with *m* or *s*

Think of each beginning sound.
Write **m** or **s**.

m   s

1. _____

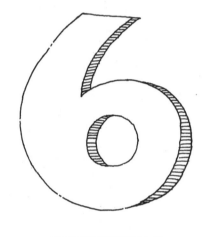

2. _____

3. _____

4. _____

5. _____

6. _____

Name _____

Words to Know

 Write a word from the box to complete each sentence.

Word Bank

go	the	on

_____

1. Go, cat, _____ !

_____

2. The cat sat _____ the mat.

_____

3. The mat sat on _____ cat.

Name _____

Begins with *c* or *t*

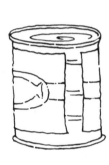 **Think of each beginning sound.**
Write c or t.

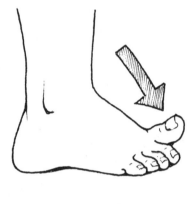

1. _____

2. _____

3. _____

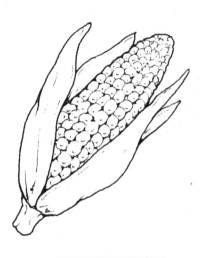

4. _____

5. _____

6. _____

Name _____

Mac the Cat Can

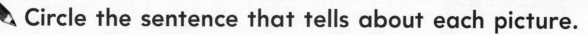

✏ **Circle the sentence that tells about each picture.**

1.

Mac the cat can get the ham.

Mac the cat is on the rug.

2.

Mac the cat can get a hug.

Mac the cat can get the bug.

3.

Mac the cat can have a nap.

Mac the cat can have jam.

Name _____

Put Them in Order!

✂ **Cut out and paste the pictures in the correct order.**

1.

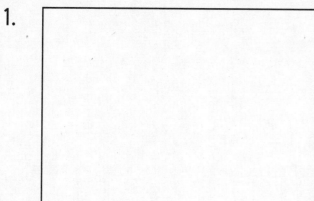

2.

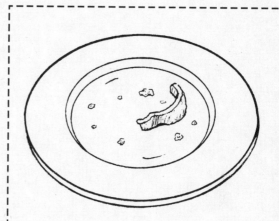

3.

Name _____

Silly Animals

 Draw a picture of an animal doing something silly.

 Write about the animal.

_____

- -

My animal is silly. It can _____

_____

- -

_____

- -

_____ .

Name _____

Begins with *n* or *f*

 Think of each beginning sound. Write *n* or *f*.

1. _____ 2. _____ 3. _____

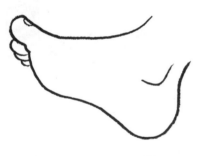 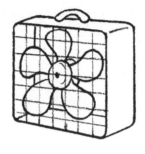 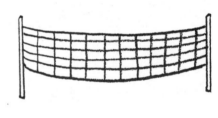

4. _____ 5. _____ 6. _____

7. _____ 8. _____ 9. _____

Name _____

Begins with *p*

Name each picture. Color the pictures that have the same beginning sound as .

Name _____

Ends with *n, f,* or *p*

✏ Name each picture. Circle the letter that stands for the ending sound.

1. n f p

2. n f p

3. n f p

4. n f p

5. n f p

6. n f p

7. n f p

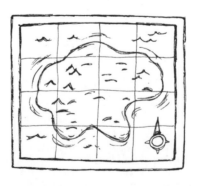

8. n f p

9. n f p

Name _____

Blending Short *a* Words

Blend the letter sounds. Then write the correct
word for each picture.

| m | a | p | | c | a | p | | c | a | t | | m | a | n |

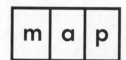

1. _____

2. _____

3. _____

4. _____

Theme 1: **All Together Now**   **51**

Name _____

Words with Short *a*

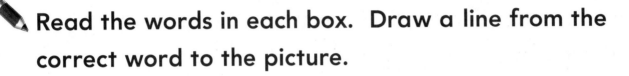 Read the words in each box. Draw a line from the correct word to the picture.

cat cap		fat fan	
pan pat		mat man	
cat cap		Pam pan	
cat can		pat pan	

Name _____

Begins with *n* or *f*

Think of each beginning sound.
Write **n** or **f**.

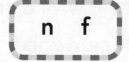

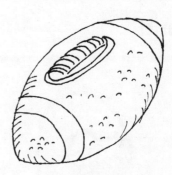

1. _____

2. _____

3. _____

4. _____

5. _____

6. _____

Name _____

Words to Know

 Write a word from the box to complete each sentence.

Word Bank

and	jump	not

_____
- - - - - - - - - - - - - - - -
1. Nan can _____ !

_____
- - - - - - - - - - - - - - - -
2. Nan _____ Pat can jump here, too.

_____
- - - - - - - - - - - - - - - -
3. We can _____ jump here.

Name _____

Words to Know

✂ Cut out and paste each sentence next to the picture it matches.

1.

2.

3.

Can we jump, too?

We can not go here.

We can jump and jump.

Name _____

Begins with *p*

Name each picture. Color the pictures whose names have the same beginning sound as .

  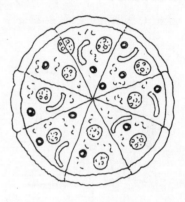

  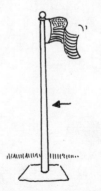

Name _____

Nan Can

 Write a word from the box to complete each sentence.

Word Bank

| school | playground | read | sing |

1. Nan can go to

_____

_____ .

2. Nan and the teacher can add

_____

_____

and _____ .

3. Nan and Fan can

_____

_____

_____ .

4. Nan and Sam go to the

_____

_____

_____ .

Name _____

Look What We Can Do!

Read each sentence. Draw a line from the picture to the sentence that tells about it.

1.

   Pam can read.

   Nat can read, too.

2.

   Pam cut a fan.

   Jen cut a cat.

3.

   Pam can go.

   Pam, Nat, and Jen can play.

Week 2

Comprehension Compare and Contrast

What's Different?

Look at both pictures. Which things in the pictures are different? Put an **X** on them.

Name _____

Things We Do at School

Write and draw about something you do at school.

Cut out your sentence and picture.

Theme 1: **All Together Now**   **61**

Name _____

Begins with *b* or *g*

Name each picture. Circle the letter that stands for the beginning sound.

1. **b g**

2. **b g**

3. **b g**

4. **b g**

5. **b g**

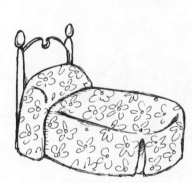

6. **b g**

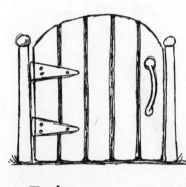

7. **b g**

8. **b g**

9. **b g**

Theme 1: **All Together Now**   63

Name _____

Begins with *h* or *r*

✏ Name each picture. Circle the letter that
stands for the beginning sound.

1. (h) r

2. (h) r

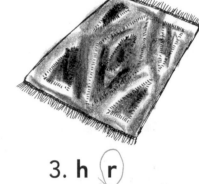

3. h (r)

4. h (r)

5. (h) r

6. (h) r

7. h (r)

8. h (r)

9. (h) r

Ends with *b, g,* or *r*

✏️ **Think of each ending sound. Write *b, g,* or *r*.**

1. _g_

2. _b_

3. _r_

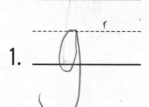

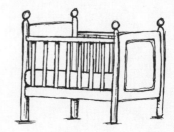

4. _r_

5. _g_

6. _b_

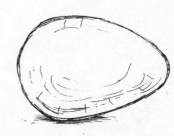

7. _b_

8. _r_

9. _g_

Theme 1: **All Together Now**   **65**

Name _____

Short *i*

Name each picture. Color the pictures whose names have the same vowel sound as  .

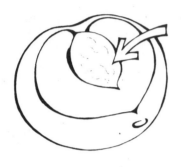 

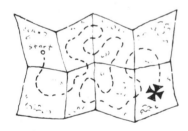  

Name _____

Blending Short *i* Words

 Blend the letter sounds. Then write the correct word for each picture.

1.

_____

- - - - - - - - - - - - -

_____

2.

_____

- - - - - - - - - - - - -

_____

3.

_____

- - - - - - - - - - - - -

_____

Week 3

Phonics Comparing Short Vowels

Short *a* and *i*

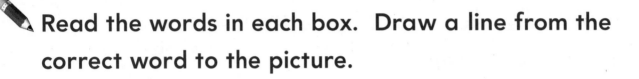 Read the words in each box. Draw a line from the correct word to the picture.

pit pig		fit fig	
big bag		pat pig	
had hit		sit bit	
fit fig		hit ham	

Name _____

Begins with *b* or *h*

Think of each beginning sound.
Write **b** or **h**.

b h

1. _____

2. _____

3. _____

4. _____

5. _____

6. _____

Name _____

Words to Know

 Write a word from the box to complete each sentence.

Word Bank

find	have	Who

_____

1. Can Pat _____ Nan?

_____

2. We _____ one pig and a cat.

_____

3. _____ can go to the mat?

Name _____

Words to Know

✂ **Cut out and paste each sentence next to the picture it matches.**

1.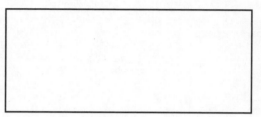

Who can find the bat?

2.

Who can jump to the hat?

3.

We have one cat and a pig.

Name _____

Begins with *r* or *g*

Think of each beginning sound.
Write r or g.

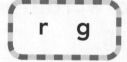

1. _____

2. _____

3. _____

4. _____

5. _____

6. _____

Theme 1: **All Together Now**   73

Name _____

A Pig in a Puddle

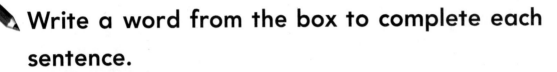 Write a word from the box to complete each sentence.

Word Bank

tub	bump	mess	mud

_____

1. The pigs hit a _____.

_____

2. The pig is in the _____.

_____

3. The pig is a _____.

_____

4. The pig is in the _____!
Goodbye!

Name _____

Three Pigs Win!

Write **Sid**, **Fig**, or **Pal** to tell about each character in **Pigs in a Rig**.

SID

1. _____ is in the mud.

PAL

2. _____ is in the jam.

FIG

3. _____ is in the bag.

Sid, Fig, and Pal win!

Theme 1: **All Together Now**   75

Name _____

What Happened?

 Look at each picture. Draw a line from the picture of what happened to the picture showing why it happened.

What happened? **Why?**

1.

2.

3.

Name _____

My Own Ending

 Draw a new ending for **Pigs in a Rig**.

Write about your new ending.

_____

_____

_____

_____

_____

Name _____

Begins with *d* or *w*

Name each picture. Circle the letter that stands for the beginning sound.

1. d w

2. d w

3. d w

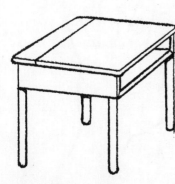

4. d w

5. d w

6. d w

7. d w

8. d w

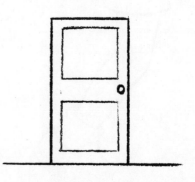

9. d w

Name _____

Begins with *l*

Name each picture. Color the pictures that have the same beginning sound as  .

Name _____

Ends with *d, l,* or *x*

✏️ **Think of each ending sound. Write *d, l,* or *x*.**

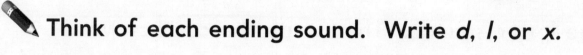

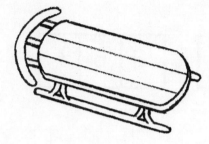

1. _____

2. _____

3. _____

4. _____

5. _____

6. _____

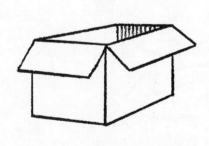

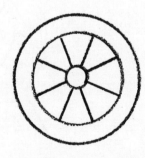

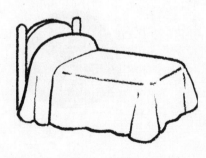

7. _____

8. _____

9. _____

Week 1

Phonics Blending Short *o*
Words

Blending Short *o* Words

 **Blend the letter sounds. Then write the correct word for each picture.**

| h | o | t | | b | o | x | | m | o | p | | d | o | t |

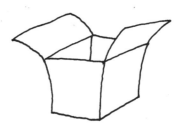

_____

- - - - - - - - - - - - - - - - - -

_____

_____

- - - - - - - - - - - - - - - - - -

_____

_____

- - - - - - - - - - - - - - - - - -

_____

_____

- - - - - - - - - - - - - - - - - -

_____

Name _____

Words with Short *o*

 Write a word from the box to complete each sentence.

Word Bank

on   fox   box

1. Go, _fox_ , go!

2. The fox sat _on_ the ox.

3. The ox sat on the _box_ !

Theme 2: **Surprise!**   83

Name _____

Short *a*, *i*, and *o*

 Write a word from the box to name each picture.

Word Bank

| map | pig | pot | dog | pat | mop |

1.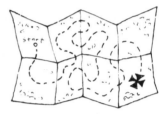

_____

- - - - - - - - - - - - - - - -

2.

_____

- - - - - - - - - - - - - - - -

3.

_____

- - - - - - - - - - - - - - - -

4.

_____

- - - - - - - - - - - - - - - -

5.

_____

- - - - - - - - - - - - - - - -

6.

_____

- - - - - - - - - - - - - - - -

Name _____

Begins with *d* or *l*

Name each picture. Think of the beginning sound. Write **d** or **l**.

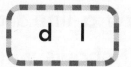

1.	2.	3.
4.	5.	6.
7.	8.	9.
10.	11.	12.

Theme 2: **Surprise!**   **85**

Name _____

Words to Know

Draw a line from each story to each picture
that shows what the story is about.

1. What have we here?

   We have one, two, three.

   We have four and five!

2. A cat can sit.

   It can sit upon a box.

   It can sit in the box, too.

3. Can the cat fit in?

   It fit in the box once.

   The cat got too big!

Name _____

Words to Know

Circle the sentence that tells about each picture.

1. One cat sat upon a box.

   We jump here.

2. Five sit.

   Three have hats.

3. A man can bat.

   Once, the four wigs fit in here.

4. What can we find?

   We have a big pan.

Name _____

Words with *w* or *x*

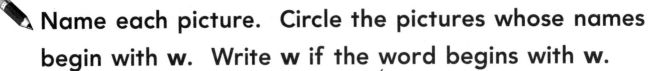 Name each picture. Circle the pictures whose names begin with **w**. Write **w** if the word begins with **w**.

1. _____ 2. _____ 3. _____

4. _____ 5. _____ 6. _____

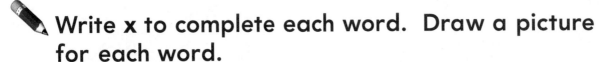 Write **x** to complete each word. Draw a picture for each word.

fo_____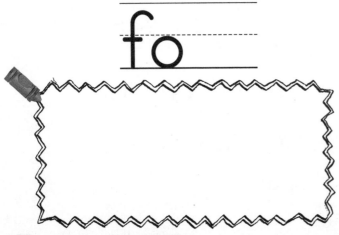

bo_____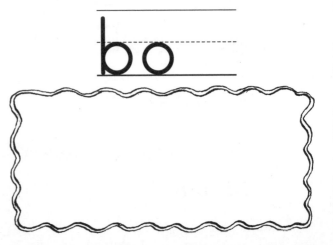

Name _____

The Surprise Party

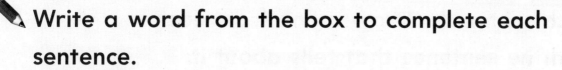 Write a word from the box to complete each sentence.

Word Bank

| candles | kids | birthday | happy |

1. **It is my** _____.
   I am sad.

2. **The** _____ **jump.**
   "Surprise!"

3. **My brother has a cake and**

   six _____.

4. **I am** _____
   at the party.

Name _____

Lots of Boxes!

Read each sentence. Draw a line from each picture to the sentence that tells about it.

1.

Tim had a flat gift.

2.

Five kids and Wag hid in the box.

3.

Dot had a big gift.

Ben had a wet gift.

4.

Name _____

Who Can Find It?

Read each sentence. Follow the directions.

Color a cat with one bat.

Color an ox in a big hat.

Name _____

Begins the Same

✂ Cut out and paste each word next to the animal whose name begins with the same sound.

1.

2.

3.

4.

hot   tan

big   fat

Begins with *y*, *k*, or *v*

Name each picture. Circle the letter that stands for the beginning sound.

1. y v k	2. k v y	3. y v k	4. v y k
5. k v y	6. k y v	7. k v y	8. y v k
9. v y k	10. k v y	11. k y v	12. y k v
13. k y v	14. k v y	15. k y v	16. y k v

Name _____

Ends with *k*

Name each picture. Write **k** if the word
ends like **look**. Write **g** if the word
ends like **big**.

Name _____

Blending Short *e* Words

Blend the letter sounds. Then write the correct word for each picture.

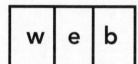 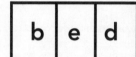 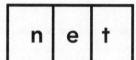 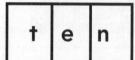

| w | e | b | | b | e | d | | n | e | t | | t | e | n |

1. _____

2. _____

3. _____

4. _____

Name _____

Words with Short e

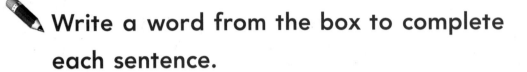 Write a word from the box to complete each sentence.

Word Bank

| ten | bed | pet | get |

_____
- - - - - - - - - - - - - -

1. I am in _____ .

_____
- - - - - - - - - - - - - -

2. We can _____ a box.

_____
- - - - - - - - - - - - - -

3. The _____ can jump in.

_____
- - - - - - - - - - - - - -

4. We have _____ cats.

Name _____

Short *a*, *e*, *i*, and *o*

Read the words in each box. Draw a line from the correct word to the picture.

pat pot		met men	
wag wig		pan pen	
ten tan	10	hit hen	
dig dog		vet vat	

Name _____

Begins with *y* or *v*

✏ **Name each picture. Think of the beginning sound. Write y or v.**

1.	2.	3.
4.	5.	6.
7.	8.	9.
10.	11.	12.

Name _____

Words to Know

Write a word from the box to complete each sentence in the story.

Word Bank

I	my	for	do

_____

1. "I have _____ bat," said Van.

_____

2. Dot said, "I _____ not have a bat."

_____

3. Van said, "The bat is _____ me.
   The bat is for you, too."

_____

4. Dot said, " ___ can hit. You can hit, too."

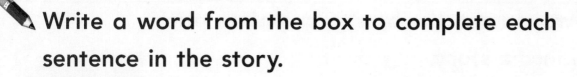

Name _____

Words to Know

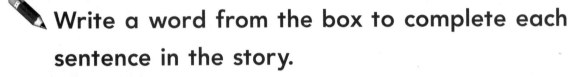

Write a word from the box to complete each sentence in the story.

Word Bank

me	is	said	you

_____
- - - - - - - - - - - -

1. "What can I do for you?" _____ the vet.

_____
- - - - - - - -

2. "My pet _____ here," I said.

_____
- - - - - - - -

3. "Can you get my pet for _____ ?" I said.

_____
- - - - - - - - - - -

4. "Here _____ go," said the vet.

Name _____

Begins with *k*

Name each picture. Color the pictures that have the same beginning sound as **kit**.

Name _____

A Bear in the Woods

✏️ Write a word from the box to complete each sentence.

Word Bank

woods   bear   snow   window

1. Dad bunny and his kids sat _____

    _____

    by the _____.

2. "You little bunnies can go play _____

    in the _____," he said.

    _____

3. "Hop in if you see the big bad _____."

4. Can you see the bear in _____

    the _____?

Name _____

Fox Runs!

Circle the word that completes each sentence. Write the word in the sentence.

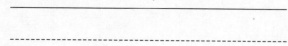

1. Kev and Viv are _____.

   bears   bunnies   cats

2. Mom said, "Fox can get you if you

   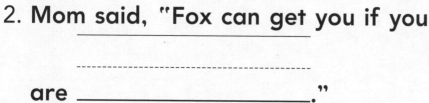

   are _____."

   little   big   sad

3. The bunnies play next to the _____.

   dog   pen   den

4. Fox sees a big snow _____.

   man   bunny   bear

   Fox runs!

Name _____

Could It Really Happen?

Look at each picture. If the picture shows something that could really happen, color it.

Name _____

An Animal Fact

 Draw a picture of an animal.

✏️ Write about the animal.

_____

- -

My animal is _____ .

_____

- -

It can _____

_____

- -

_____ .

108   Theme 2: **Surprise!**

Name _____

Begins with *qu*, *j*, or *z*

Name each picture. Circle the letter that stands for the beginning sound.

1.	2.	3.	4.
j qu z	z qu j	qu j z	j z qu

5.	6.	7.	8.
j z qu	j qu z	j z qu	qu j z

9.	10.	11.	12.
j qu z	z qu j	z j qu	z qu j

13.	14.	15.	16.
z j qu	z j qu	qu j z	z qu j

Name _____

Short *u*

 Name each picture. Color the pictures whose names have the same vowel sound as 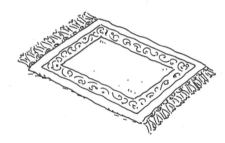 .

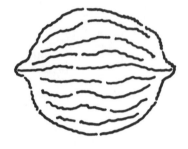

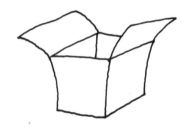

Name _____

Blending Short *u* Words

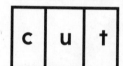 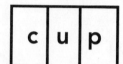 Blend the letter sounds. Then write the correct word for each picture.

| c | u | t | | c | u | p | | b | u | g | | r | u | g |

1.

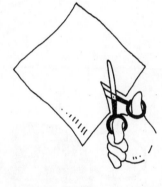

_____
- - - - - - - - - - - - - - - - - -
_____

2.

_____
- - - - - - - - - - - - - - - - - -
_____

3.

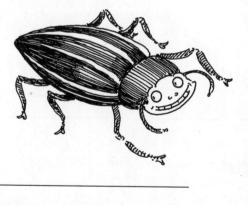

_____
- - - - - - - - - - - - - - - - - -
_____

4.

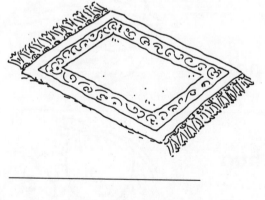

_____
- - - - - - - - - - - - - - - - - -
_____

Name _____

Short *a*, *e*, *i*, *o*, and *u*

Read the words in each box. Draw a line from the correct word to the picture.

jet		rug	
jug		rig	
bug		mat	
bag		mug	
nut		hit	
not		hut	
hug		cut	
hog		cat	

Name ________________________

Begins with *j* or *z*

Name each picture. Think of the beginning sound. Write j or z.

j z

1. 
___

2. 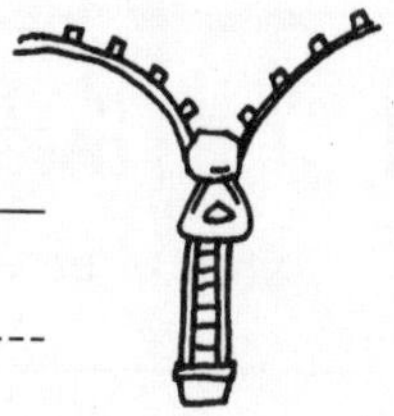
___

3. 
___

4. 
___

5. 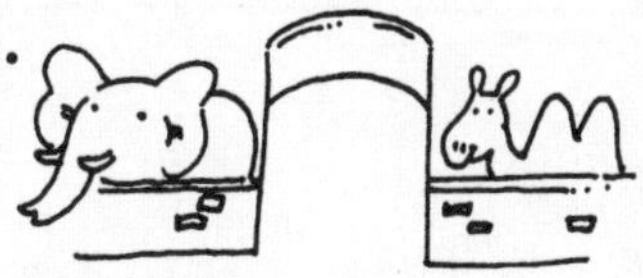
___

6. 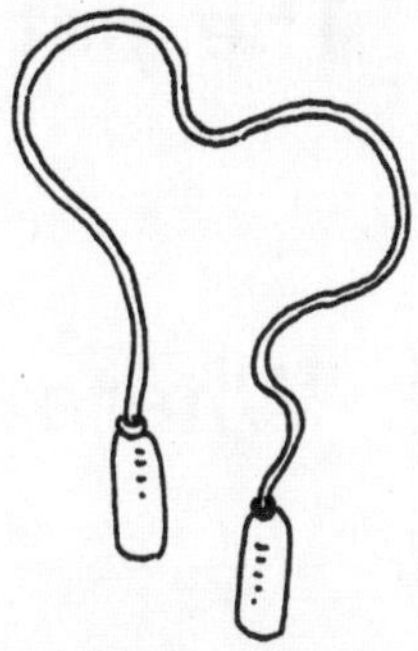
___

7. 
___

8. 
___

9. 
___

10. 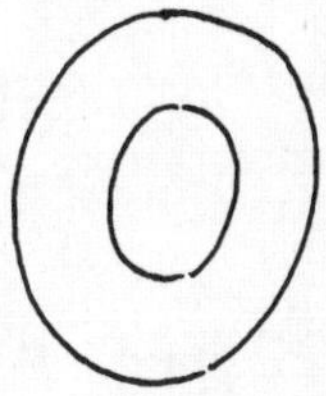
___

11. 
___

12. 
___

Name _____

Words to Know

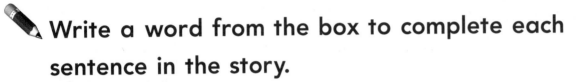 Write a word from the box to complete each sentence in the story.

Word Bank

does   away   pull   live   are   they

1. The pet can get _____ .

2. Where _____ the pet go?

3. He can _____ the mat.

4. Can _____ find the pet?

5. They _____ wet.

6. The pet can _____ here!

Name _____

Words to Know

✂ Cut out and paste each sentence under the picture it matches.

1.

2.

3.

Where are Pat and Dan?
Pat and Dan go away.

Where do Dot and Jan live?
They pull in here.

Does Ken live here?
He does!

Name _____

Begins with *qu*

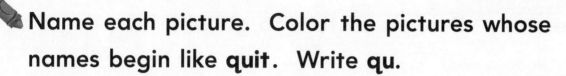

Name each picture. Color the pictures whose names begin like **quit**. Write **qu**.

1.	2.	3.
4.	5.	6.
7.	8.	9.

Name _____

Bugs in the Pool

Read the story. Draw a picture to go with it.

Bud Bug and Pat Bug sit in the sun. They are hot! They jump on a leaf in a pool. They get wet. They are not hot!

Name _____

What's Next?

✂ Cut out and paste the sentences in the order that they were said in the story.

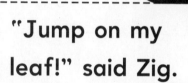

1.

2.

3.

4.

"Jump on my leaf!" said Zig.

"We quit, too!" said Zag and Kip.

"I see a pool," Zig said.

"We are in a jug!" said Zig.

Week 3

Comprehension Story
Structure

Name _____

Think of the Story

 Think about A Surprise for Zig Bug. Answer the questions.

Who? _____

Where? _____

What is the problem? _____

How is the problem solved? _____

Name _____

What a Bug!

 Draw a picture of a bug.

 Write about the bug.

_____
- -

My bug is _____ .

_____
- -

It has _____

_____
- -

_____ .

Name __Ben__

Double Final Consonants

Read each sentence. Circle the word that
ends with a double consonant and write it
below.

1. It is (fall).

2. Do we have a (bass) yet?

3. We can (add) to
the can.

4. We have to (fill) the can!

1. __fall__

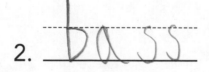

2. __bass__

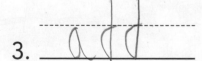

3. __add__

4. __fill__

Theme 3: **Let's Look Around!**   **123**

Name _____

Ending Sounds

✏️ Write a word from the box to complete each sentence in the story.

Word Bank

sat	pack	is	has	bag

_____

Jack has to _____ .

Can Mack fit in the _____ ?

Jack _____ to go.

Mack _____ in the back.

Jack sat. Mack _____ .

They can go!

Name _____

More Than One

Read each sentence. Circle the picture of the underlined word.

1. **Where are the animals?**

2. **Ben has cats.**

3. **Nan has hens.**

4. **Kit has a pig.**

Name _____

Words to Know

Write a word from the box to complete each sentence in the story.

Word Bank

animal	full	see	flower

It Is Cold

"Look!" said Zack.

_____

"I _____ a bird."

"Look!" said Jack.

_____

"I see an _____ ."

_____

It is _____ of nuts."

"Look!" said Pat.

_____

"I have a fall _____ here."

Name _____

Words to Know

Look at the picture. Then read each question and circle the answer.

1. **Where is the animal?**

2. **Where is the bird?**

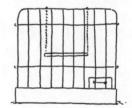

3. **What is full of nuts?**

4. **Who has the flower?**

Theme 3: **Let's Look Around!**   **129**

Name _____

Different Seasons

Write a word from the box to complete each sentence in the story.

Word Bank

| trees | summer | winter | rain |

1. The bear can nap in _____.
   The birds can go south.

2. It is fall.
   Leaves fall off the _____.

3. In spring, it can _____.

4. It can be hot in the _____.
   Insects buzz in the hot sun.

Name _____

What Season Is It?

✂ Cut out and paste the sentences under the picture they tell about.

It can get wet.	It can get cold.
We can see flowers.	The animals can nap.
A lot of leaves fall.	It can get hot.
Animals find twigs and nuts.	Ducks swim and bugs buzz!

Theme 3: **Let's Look Around!**   **131**

Name _____

What's It All About?

Read **Big Cats.** Then look at the chart. The topic and main idea are filled in. You add the details.

super!

Big Cats

What can big cats do?

Big cats can jump.

Big cats can sit, too.

Big cats can live in dens.

Big cats are not pets!

Topic	Big cats
Main Idea	A big cat can do a lot.
Details	A big cat can sit.
	A big cat can jump.
	A big cat lives in dens.
	A big cat are not pets.

Theme 3: **Let's Look Around!**   **133**

Name _____

The Short *a* Sound

 Write a word from the box to complete each sentence in the story.

an

at

can

cat

had

man

_____

1. My pet is _____ animal.

_____

2. It is a _____ .

_____

3. A _____ let me have the cat.

_____

4. He _____ a lot of cats.

_____

5. My cat _____ do a lot.

_____

6. Look _____ my cat jump!

Name _____

Make a Sentence

Draw a line from the part of the sentence that names a person or object to the part of the sentence that tells what the person or object can do.

1. We   can live in a den.

2. A fox   can go to school.

Write the sentences you made.

1. We can go to school.

2. A fox can live in a den.

Name **Bou**

Spelling Spree

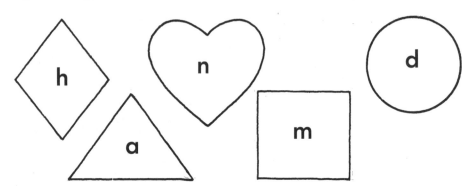

Use the letter shapes to write three Spelling Words.

1. <u>man</u>   2. <u>had</u>   3. <u>an</u>

Proofread each sentence. Circle each Spelling Word that is wrong, and write it correctly.

4. I see a big (kat.) <u>cat</u>

5. Look (ad) it go! <u>at</u>

6. It (ken) jump, too. <u>can</u>

Week 1

Writing Writing About Favorite Seasons

Name

Which Season Is Your Favorite?

Write about your favorite season.

Season Spring

is nise becouse

it has fluors.

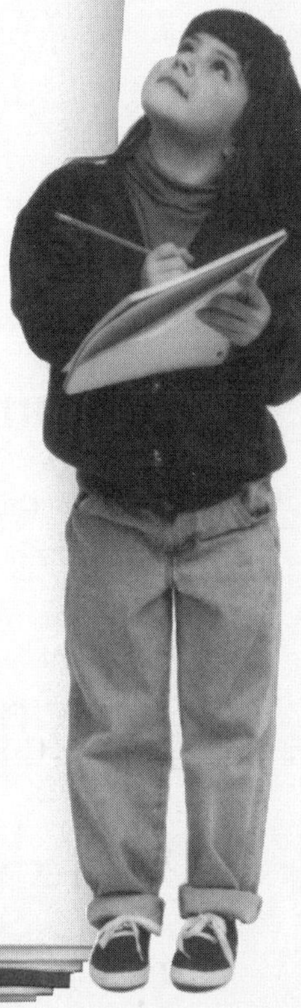

Name _____

Verb Endings -s, -ed, -ing

✏️ **Read each sentence. Circle the sentence that tells about each picture.**

1. **Nan is looking for Jill to play.**

   Ken looks for a bug.

2. **Nan kicked the can.**

   Nan sees Jill.

3. **Nan is going to dig.**

   Nan is going to jump.

4. **Nan and Jill jumped.**

   Nan and Pat filled the box.

Name _____

Words with Short *i*

Name each picture. Write **i** if the picture name has the short **i** sound.

1.	2.	3.	4.
5.	6.	7.	8.
9.	10.	11.	12.
13.	14.	15.	16.

Name _____

Words with Short *i*

✏ **Read each sentence, and circle the picture of the underlined word. Write the word.**

1. **Ben is <u>six</u>.**

_____
- - - - - - - - - - -
_____

2. **He is looking for a <u>mitt</u>.**

_____
- - - - - - - - - - -
_____

3. **The <u>wig</u> is not for Ben.**

_____
- - - - - - - - - - -
_____

4. **The <u>bib</u> fits Meg.**

_____
- - - - - - - - - - -
_____

5. **The cap is for <u>him</u>.**

_____
- - - - - - - - - - -
_____

140 Theme 3: **Let's Look Around!**

Name _____

Whose Is It?

Write the words from the box under the picture they name.

| ✓ Jill's box |
| ✓ Bill's cat |
| ✓ Lin's hat |
| Rick's mitt |

1.

Lin's hat

2.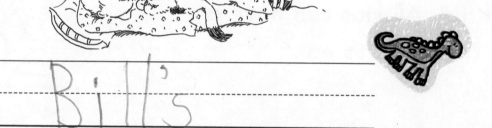

Bill's

3.

Jill's box

4.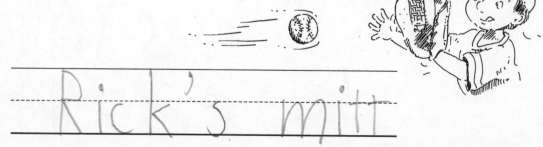

Rick's mitt

Theme 3: **Let's Look Around!** 141

Name _____

Words to Know

Draw a line from each sentence to the picture it tells about.

1. Bill got the paper first.

2. "Look at the paper, Dad!"
   said Bill.
   The paper said, "Come eat
   at Kit's! All kids can have a
   dip and a bit to eat."

3. "Shall I call Kit's?" said Bill.
   "I have never had a dip at
   Kit's."

4. "Why not?" said Dad.
   "Every kid will go. Get set."

Name _____

Words to Know

Circle the sentence that tells about each picture.

1.

"Why do we jump?" said Dot Hen.

"Look at the paper first," said Dot Hen.

2.

"Call all the hens to eat," it said.

"I never see all the animals," said Fox.

3.

"Every flower looks tan," said Fox.

"Shall I call Pig to eat, too?" said Dot Hen.

Name _____

An Ice Cream Cone

Write a word from the box to complete each sentence. Use the pictures to help you.

Word Bank

| cone | try | napkin | shop |

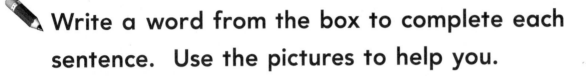

1. We go to the ice cream _____.

2. Shall I get a dish or a _____?

3. I shall _____ the green

kind in a cone. It is mint.

4. I wish I had a _____.

Name _____

What a Mess!

Read each question. Circle the correct answer.

1. **Who had an ice cream shop?**
   Miss Jill had an ice cream shop.
   Jack and Bill had an ice cream shop.

2. **What did Jack get to eat?**
   Jack got ice cream in a dish.
   Jack got ice cream in a cone.

3. **What did Bill get to eat?**
   Bill got green ice cream.
   Bill got plum ice cream and nuts.

4. **What fell on all the animals?**
   Ice cream fell on all the animals.
   Napkins fell on all the animals.

5. **Who helped Miss Jill?**
   Jack and Bill helped Miss Jill.
   All the animals helped Miss Jill.

Name _____

What Happens Next?

✂ Cut out and paste a picture to show what happens next.

1.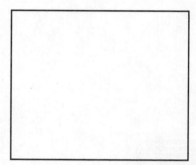

2.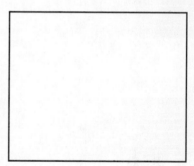

Theme 3: **Let's Look Around!** **147**

Name _____

Spelling Spree

Write the missing letter to complete each
Spelling Word. Then write the word.

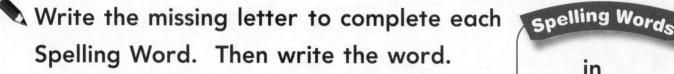

Spelling Words

in
it
him
big
sit
did

1. d___d _____

2. h___m _____

3. ___t _____

Proofread each sentence. Circle each Spelling
Word that is wrong, and write it correctly.

4. The pig is bige. _____

5. The pig is en a pen! _____

6. The pig can zit. _____

Week 2

Writing Describing Favorite
Foods

Name _____

Your Favorite Food

Write sentences to describe your favorite food.

What is your favorite food?

_____

_____

_____

_____

What does it look like?

_____

_____

_____

_____

How does it taste?

_____

_____

_____

_____

Clusters with *r*

Name each picture. Circle the letters that stand for the beginning sounds.

1.	2.	3.	4.
(cr) pr fr	fr (br) tr	br gr tr	(pr) gr tr

5.	6.	7.	8.
br cr (tr)	br dr (fr)	(br) gr tr	cr dr (tr)

9.	10.	11.	12.
cr (fr) pr	cr pr (fr)	(br) dr pr	br fr (pr)

13.	14.	15.	16.
(br) fr pr	(cr) pr fr	(dr) fr pr	tr fr (dr)

Name _Ben_

Clusters with *r*

 Circle the word that names each picture.
Write the word.

1.

   brick   **brim**

   brick

2.

   grab   **grass**

   grass

3.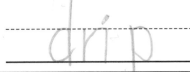

   drag   **drip**

   drip

4.

   crib   **crab**

   crib

5.

   trap   **trip**

   trap

6.

   crack   **crab**

   crab

Name _____

Contractions with *'s*

Rewrite each sentence. Use a word from the
box in place of the underlined words.

Word Bank

He's	It's	What's	Where's	Who's

1. <u>Who is</u> calling you?

_____

- -

_____

2. <u>He is</u> my dad.

_____

- -

_____

3. <u>Where is</u> my hat?

_____

- -

_____

4. <u>What is</u> in the box?

_____

- -

_____

5. <u>It is</u> Dad's hat!

_____

- -

_____

Theme 3: **Let's Look Around!** 155

Name _____

Words to Know

 Read the story. Color the picture that matches the story.

"Look!" said Kris. "I see many animals!"

"Me, too!" said Brad.

Kris said, "I see some green and brown frogs!"

"Me, too!" said Brad.

Kris said, "I also see a bird as blue as my cap!"

"Me, too," said Brad.

"I like to look at the colors of all the pets," said Kris.

"Me, too!" said the bird.

"Funny bird!" said Brad.

Name _____

Words to Know

Read the words in the box. Write the words that name colors on the fish. Write the other words on the boat.

Word Bank

also

blue

brown

color

funny

green

like

many

some

Who Am I?

Write a word from the box to complete each riddle. Use the pictures to help you.

Word Bank

| dolphins | otter | sea horse | fish |

1. I have gills to breathe.

   _____

   \- - - - - - - - - - - - - - - - - -

   I am a _____ .

2. I can swim on my back.

   _____

   \- - - - - - - - - - - - - - - - - -

   I am an _____ .

3. We play in the sea.

   _____

   \- - - - - - - - - - - - - - - - - -

   We are _____ .

4. I can grab with my tail.

   _____

   \- - - - - - - - - - - - - - - - - -

   I am a _____ .

Name _____

What Did You See?

✂ Read each question. Cut out and paste the correct answer under the question.

1. **What can grab?**

2. **What do fish eat?**

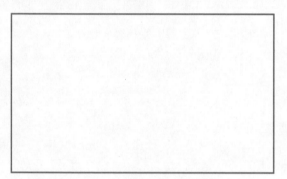

3. **Where's the funny fish?**

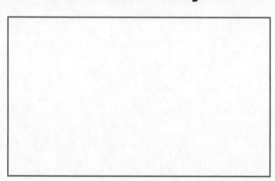

Some fish eat plants.

Here's the funny fish!

A sea horse can grab.

Theme 3: **Let's Look Around!** **159**

Name _____

Make Them Complete!

Write an action part from the box to complete each sentence in the story.

gets a bass   jump   eat   fix the fish

1. Some fish _____ .

2. Mom _____ .

3. Dad and the kids _____ .

4. Then they _____ !

Name _____

Plan Your Trip!

Write your ideas about your trip.

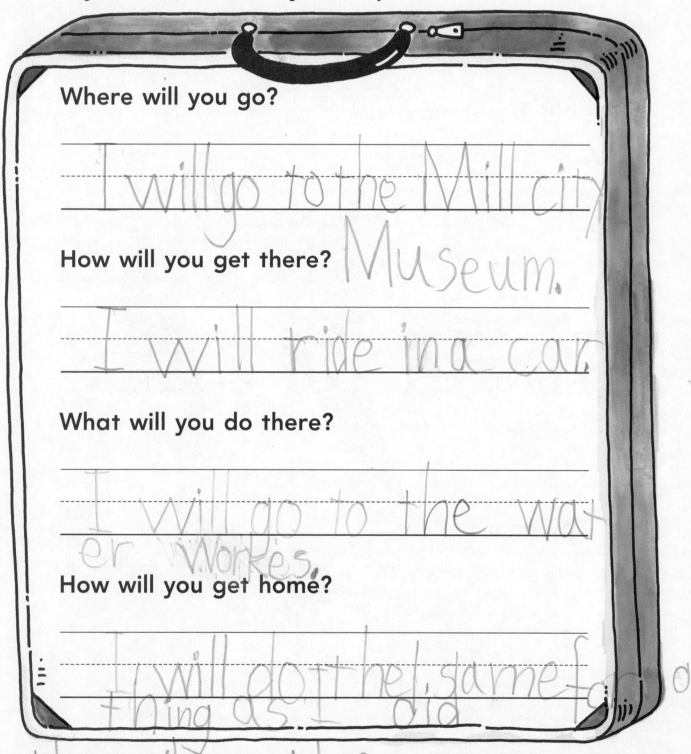

Where will you go?

I will go to the Mill city
Museum.

How will you get there?

I will ride in a car.

What will you do there?

I will go to the wat
er workes.

How will you get home?

I will do the same
thing as I did on
the whay there.

Theme 3: **Let's Look Around!**   165

Name _____

Clusters with *l*

Name each picture. Circle the letters that stand for the beginning sounds.

1. cr (cl) bl

2. sl gr (gl)

3. fr (fl) sl

4. (pl) pr cl

5. (sl) cl fl

6. gl (fl) sl

7. (gl) gr pl

8. pr sl (pl)

9. (cl) pl cr

10. (bl) pl gl

11. (bl) br sl

12. sl pl (cl)

13. fr (fl) sl

14. cl gl (pl)

15. cr (sl) bl

16. (gl) gr cl

Name _____

Clusters with *l*

Circle the word that names each picture.
Write the word.

1. flat
    (flag)

    flag

2. (clock)
    class

    clock

3. (glass)
    grass

    glass

4. (block)
    blot

    block

5. (plug)
    slug

    plug

6. (sled)
    slacks

    sled

7. flap
    (clap)

    clap

8. (flat)
    flip

    flip

Name _____

Words with Short o

✏ Name each picture. Write **o** if the picture
name has the short **o** sound.

1.	2.	3.	4.
5.	6.	7.	8.
9.	10.	11.	12.
13.	14.	15.	16.

Name _____

Words with Short *o*

Read each sentence, and circle the picture of the underlined word. Write the word.

1. <u>Dot</u> can pack for a trip.

_____

2. Bob sees a <u>clock</u>.

_____

3. See Dot's <u>doll</u>.

_____

4. See Dot's <u>socks</u>.

_____

5. See Dot's <u>blocks</u>.

_____
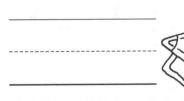 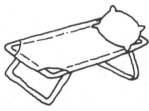  

Name _____

Words to Know

✂ Cut out the pictures. Paste each picture
above the sentence that goes with it.

1.

"Come here and see my
pictures," said Jan.

2.

Here is a picture of six
people.

3.

See the mother and
father hug the children.

4.

I love the picture of
your family.

Theme 4: **Family and Friends**   **171**

Name _____

Words to Know

Write a word from the box to complete each sentence in the story.

Word Bank

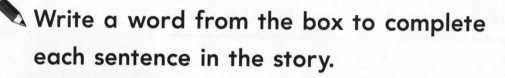

| your | love | picture | children |

Come see the people in my family.

_____

Here is a _____.

We have a mother, a father, and

_____

two _____.

_____

We get lots of _____.

_____

Who's in _____ family?

Name _____

Go Away, Rex!

Write a word from the box to complete each sentence.

Word Bank

sorry	pillows	visit	clean

_____

1. Tim and Rex went to _____ Ben.

_____

2. Rex jumped on Ben's _____.

_____

3. Rex sat on Ben's _____ rug.

_____

4. "I am _____!" said Tim.

Name _____

Who Said It?

Draw a line from each person to what they said in the story.

1. "I am sorry I yelled at you."

2. "Here are the children I love."

3. "Otto is not helping."

4. "Let's clean up for Gran's visit."

5. "OK. You can help me play!"

Dad

Otto

Fred

Gran

Name _____

Drawing Conclusions

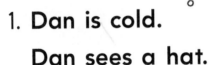 **Read the sentences. Write your conclusion.**

1. Dan is cold.

  Dan sees a hat.

  _____
  -

Dan will _____

  _____
  -
  _____

2. The vet looks at the pet.

  The pet is not sick.

  _____
  -

The pet will _____

  _____
  -
  _____

Name _____

The Short *o* Sound

Write a word to complete each sentence.

Spelling Words

on	not	got	box	hot	top

_____

1. It is _____.

2. Tom _____ a big box.

3. See what he did to the _____!

4. The box is _____ Bob.

5. It is on _____ of Bob.

6. It's _____ hot in the box.

Theme 4: **Family and Friends**   177

Name _____

Make It a Sentence!

 Write a naming part to complete each sentence.

> The cat   Kim

1. _____ likes to kick and pass.

2. _____ likes to sit in Kim's lap.

 Write an action part to complete each sentence.

> lives in a den   gets a job

3. Dad _____.

4. The fox _____.

Name _____

Spelling Spree

Write the missing letter. Write the word.

Spelling Words

on	not	got	box	hot	top

1. h __ t _____

2. g __ t _____   3. n __ t _____

Proofread each sentence. Circle each Spelling Word that is wrong, and write it correctly.

4. I have a big bocks. _____

5. Fran and I sit un it. _____

6. The tp falls in! _____

Name _____

What Is Your Answer?

Write a complete sentence to
answer each question.

1. Who is in your family?

_____

- -

_____

- -

_____

- -

_____

2. What fun does your family have?

_____

- -

_____

- -

_____

- -

_____

Name _____

Clusters with *s*

Name each picture. Circle the letters that
stand for the beginning sounds.

1.	2.	3.	4.
sc sl st	st sl sp	sp sm sl	st sm sp
5.	6.	7.	8.
sn sw sp	sl sw st	sl st sp	st sl sc
9.	10.	11.	12.
sc sn st	sk sp sw	sw st sl	sl sw sm
13.	14.	15.	16.
st sw sl	sn sl sp	st sk sl	sm sp sk

Theme 4: **Family and Friends**   **181**

Name _____

Clusters with *s*

Read each word. Write **s** before each word.
Read the new word.

1. ___led	2. ___tick	3. ___nap
4. ___cat	5. ___pin	6. ___top
7. ___pot	8. ___kid	9. ___lip
10. ___mock	11. ___well	12. ___tack

Name _____

Words with Short *e*

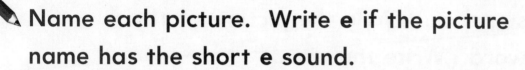

Name each picture. Write **e** if the picture
name has the short **e** sound.

1.	2.	3.	4.
5.	6.	7.	8.
9.	10.	11.	12.
13.	14.	15.	16.

Theme 4: **Family and Friends**   **183**

Name _____

Words with Short *e*

Read each sentence. Circle the picture of the underlined word. Write the word.

1. The bird has a <u>nest</u>.

_____
- - - - - - - - - - -
_____

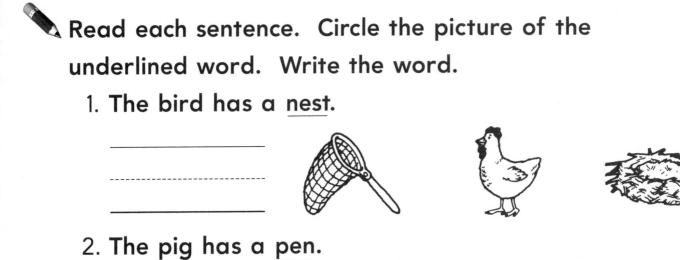

2. The pig has a <u>pen</u>.

_____
- - - - - - - - - - -
_____

3. The bug has a <u>web</u>.

_____
- - - - - - - - - - -
_____

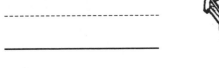 

4. The cub has a <u>den</u>.

_____
- - - - - - - - - - -
_____

5. Pat has a <u>bed</u>.

_____
- - - - - - - - - - -
_____

Name _____

Silent Letters in *kn*, *wr*, *gn*

Name each picture. Circle the pair of letters that begin each picture name. Write the two letters.

1.

wr   kn

_____

_ _ _ _ _ _ _ _ _

2.

wr   kn

_____

_ _ _ _ _ _ _ _ _

3.

wr   kn

_____

_ _ _ _ _ _ _ _ _

4.

wr   kn

_____

_ _ _ _ _ _ _ _ _

5.

gn   wr

_____

_ _ _ _ _ _ _ _ _

6.

gn   wr

_____

_ _ _ _ _ _ _ _ _

7.

wr   gn

_____

_ _ _ _ _ _ _ _ _

8.

kn   wr

_____

_ _ _ _ _ _ _ _ _

9.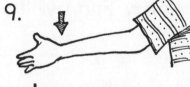

kn   wr

_____

_ _ _ _ _ _ _ _ _

Name _____

Words to Know

Write words from the box to complete the story.

Word Bank

sing   read   today   play

Fran is my best friend.

_____

She can _____ like a bird.

_____

She can _____ tricks, too.

_____

I will write to Fran _____

I will tell my best friend what I did.

I know Fran will write back.

_____

I can _____ what she did, too!

Name _____

Words to Know

✂ Cut out and paste each sentence next to the picture it describes.

1.

2.

3.

I will write to Jan!

We can read, sing, and play.

Today I met a girl. I know she is my friend.

Name _____

Jill's New Dog

 Write a word from the box to complete each sentence.

Word Bank

| smile | sign | Dear | books |

_____

_____ Bob,

My new dog, Bud, makes me _____.

I like to read _____ about dogs.

I made a _____ for Bud's house.

Bud's Dog House

Your friend,

Jill

Name _____

Put Them in Order

 **Think about Two Best Friends.** Cut out the pictures and sentences. Paste them in order.

1	2	3

Peg meets a new friend.

Peg writes a letter to her old friend.

Peg's dad packs boxes.

Alike and Different

Think about Peg and Flower in **Two Best Friends**. Read each phrase in the box. Write it in the chart where it belongs.

can jump	can play	can not read
can write	can not write	can read

Peg   **Both**   **Flower**

Name _____

The Short *e* Sound

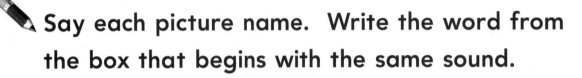 Say each picture name. Write the word from the box that begins with the same sound.

Spelling Words

get   ten   red   pet   men   yes

1.

_____

2.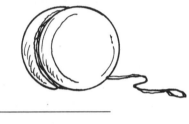

_____

3.

_____

4.

_____

5.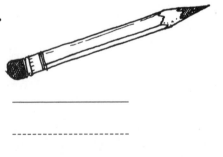

_____

6.

_____

Name _____

Find the Sentence

Read each group of words. Underline each telling sentence.

Mom calls to me.

Mom

Bob sings.

sings

Dad looks at the paper.

looks at the paper

wins the prize

Bob wins the prize.

Name _____

Spelling Spree

Write the Spelling Words that rhyme with **pen** under the 🖊. Write the Spelling Words that rhyme with **jet** under the ✈.

Spelling Words

| get | ten | red | pet | men | yes |

pen

_____

1. _____

3. _____

jet

_____

2. _____

4. _____

Proofread each sentence. Circle each Spelling Word that is wrong, and write it correctly.

5. I like the color redd. _____

6. I said yez. _____

Name _____

Write About It!

✏️ **Choose a topic. Then write some sentences about it.**

Topic:

_____

- -

_____

- -

_____

Sentences:

_____

- -

_____

- -

_____

- -

_____

- -

_____

Name _____

Triple Clusters

Read the story. Write each word in dark print next to the picture it names.

Big Gus **splits** the logs.
The **scraps** go in the bin.
Big Gus **scrubs** up.
He **strums** and hums.

1. _____

2. _____

3. _____

4. _____

Name _____

Words with Short *u*

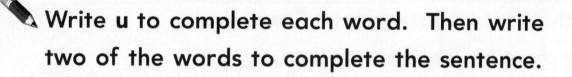 Write **u** to complete each word. Then write
two of the words to complete the sentence.

1. b___s

2. dr___m

3. f___n

4. t___b

5. d___ck

6. j___st

7. The _____ swims in the _____ .

Theme 4: **Family and Friends** 197

Name _____

Words with Short *u*

Read each word in dark print. Circle and
write the rhyming word in the box.

bug	tug	**fun**	but
_____	sun	_____	luck
_____	cub	_____	run
nut	hum	**buzz**	slug
_____	cut	_____	rug
_____	duck	_____	fuzz
gum	club	**dust**	must
_____	plum	_____	hug
_____	puff	_____	jump

Name _____

Words to Know

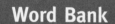 Write words from the box to complete the story.

Word Bank

Would   walk   hold   hear   hurt

_____

1. My dog is _____.

_____

2. We _____ the vet can help us learn why.

_____

3. I have to _____ my dog in the car.

_____

4. At the vet's, we _____ down the steps.

_____

5. _____ the vet help my dog?

Words to Know

Read the story. Draw a picture to go with it.

My funny cat can learn to walk.
She falls down, but she does
not get hurt.
I do not hear Mom and Dad.
My cat hears their steps.
When we go in the car, I hold my cat.
Would you like to see my cat?

Name _____

Stay, Buzz!

Write a word from the box to complete each sentence.

Word Bank

street

leash

face

chase

Miss Webb said, "Stay, Buzz. I will put

_____

_____

on your _____."

Buzz saw a cat. He had to

_____

_____

_____ it!

Buzz pulled Miss Webb down

_____

_____

the _____.

_____

_____

Buzz licked Miss Webb's _____.
She said, "I love you, Buzz, but you have to go
to dog school!"

Theme 4: **Family and Friends**   **201**

Name _____

Spritz

 **Circle the word that completes each sentence.**

1. Spritz liked to chase Miss Duff's _____.

   cat   car   pig

2. Spritz dug up Mom's _____.

   leash   funny   flowers

3. Spritz went to a school for _____.

   down   dogs   tubs

4. Spritz learned to sit and _____!

   stay   sad   go

Put Them in Order

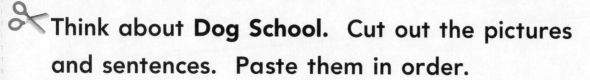

✂ Think about **Dog School.** Cut out the pictures
and sentences. Paste them in order.

1   **2**   **3**

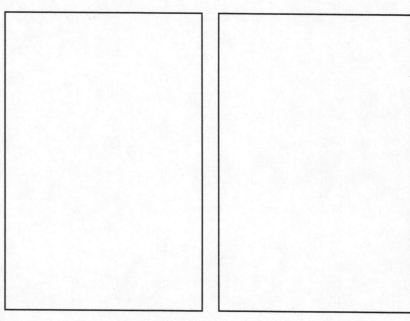

Spritz passed
the test!

Spritz likes to
chase the car.

Spritz did not
do well in class.

✂

Name _____

The Short *u* Sound

Read each clue. Write the correct Spelling
Word from the box.

Spelling Words

| up | us | but | fun | cut | run |

1. not walk:

_____

- - - - - - - - - - -

_____

2. not down:

_____

- - - - - - - - - - -

_____

3. like we:

_____

- - - - - - - - - - -

_____

4. what tricks are:

_____

- - - - - - - - - - -

_____

Write the two words that rhyme with hut.

5. _____

- - - - - - - - - - -

_____

6. _____

- - - - - - - - - - -

_____

Theme 4: **Family and Friends** **205**

Name _____

Where's the Question?

Read each sentence. Underline each asking sentence.

1. The class play is today.

   What day is it?

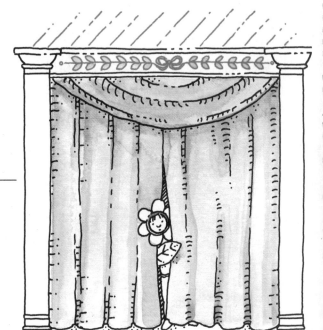

2. Who is in the play?

   The play has animals.

3. Can we go to the play?

   I can write a play.

4. The play is fun.

   Where is the next play?

Name _____

Spelling Spree

 Use the letter shapes to make Spelling Words.

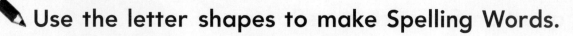
Spelling Words

| up | us | but | fun | cut | run |

1. _____

2. _____

3. _____

 Proofread each sentence. Circle each Spelling Word that is wrong, and write it correctly.

_____

4. I like to runn. _____

5. It is a lot of fon. _____

6. I can run ub a hill. _____

Theme 4: **Family and Friends** **207**

Name _____

What's Your Question?

 Write a question for each question word.

_____

1. **Who** _____

_____

2. **What** _____

_____

3. **Where** _____

_____

4. **Why** _____

_____

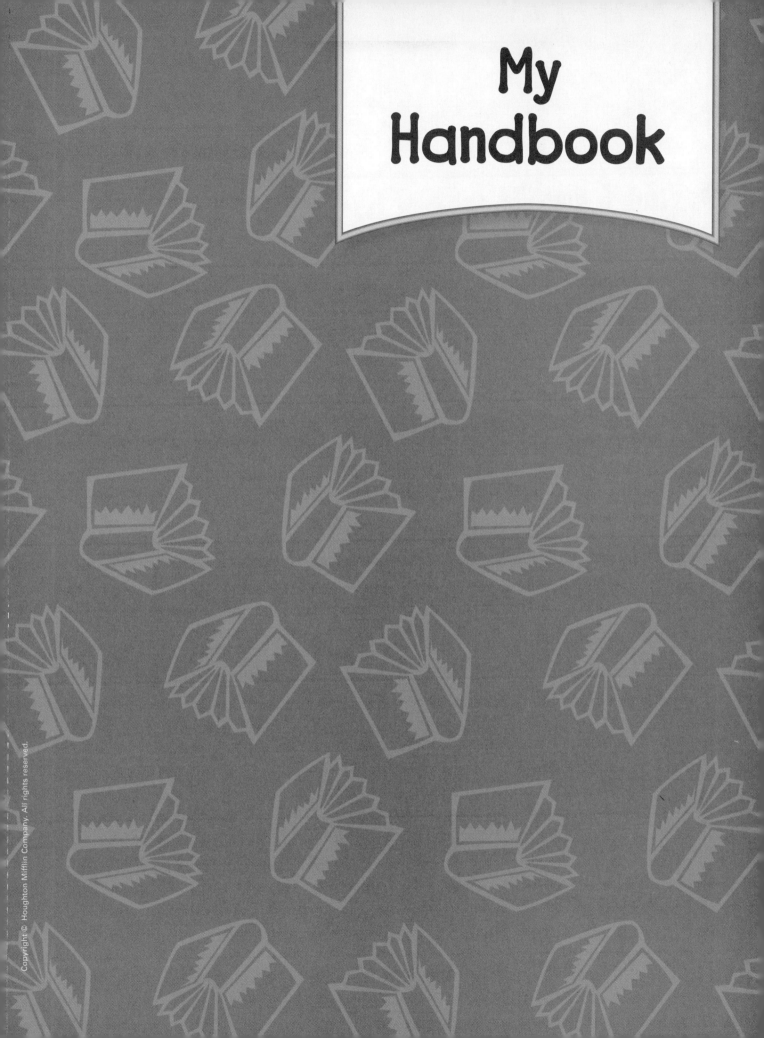

My Handbook

210

Contents

Andy Apple

Benny Bear

Callie Cat

Dudley Duck

Edna Elephant

Fifi Fish

Gertie Goose

Hattie Horse

Iggy Iguana

Jumping Jill

Keely Kangaroo

Larry Lion

Mimi Mouse

Nyle Noodle

Ozzie Octopus

Pippa Pig

Queenie Queen

Reggie Rooster

Sammy Seal

Tiggy Tiger

Umbie Umbrella

Vinny Volcano

Willy Worm

Mr. X-Ray

Yetta Yo-Yo

Zelda Zebra

1. **Look at the letters from left to right.**

2. **Think about the sounds for the letters, and look for word parts you know.**

3. **Blend the sounds to read the word.**

4. **Ask yourself: Is it a word I know? Does it make sense in what I am reading?**

5. **If not, ask yourself: What else can I try?**

Predict/Infer

► Think about the title, the illustrations, and what you have read so far.

► Tell what you think will happen next or what you will learn.

Question

► Ask yourself questions as you read.

Monitor/Clarify

► Ask yourself if what you are reading makes sense.

► If you don't understand something, reread, read ahead, or use the illustrations.

Summarize

► Think about the main ideas or the important parts of the story.

► Tell the important things in your own words.

Evaluate

► Ask yourself: Do I like what I have read? Am I learning what I wanted to know?

Writing the Alphabet

Trace and write the letters.

Aa Aa

Bb Bb

Cc Cc

Dd Dd

Ee Ee

Ff Ff

Gg Gg

Trace and write the letters.

Hh Hh

Ii Ii

Jj Jj

Kk Kk

Ll Ll

Mm Mm

Trace and write the letters.

Nn Nn

Oo Oo

Pp Pp

Qq Qq

Rr Rr

Ss Ss

Tt Tt

Trace and write the letters.

Uu Uu

Vv Vv

Ww Ww

Xx Xx

Yy Yy

Zz Zz

Trace and write the letters.

Aa Aa

Bb Bb

Cc Cc

Dd Dd

Ee Ee

Ff Ff

Gg Gg

Trace and write the letters.

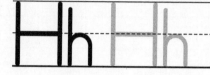

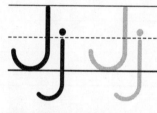

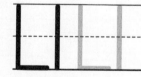

Trace and write the letters.

Nn Nn

Oo Oo

Pp Pp

Qq Qq

Rr Rr

Ss Ss

Tt Tt

Trace and write the letters.

U u U u

V v V v

W w W w

X x X x

Y y Y y

Z z Z z

How to Study a Word

1. **LOOK** at the word.

2. **SAY** the word.

3. **THINK** about the word.

4. **WRITE** the word.

5. **CHECK** the spelling.

A

a

about

again

always

and

any

around

as

B

back

because

before

C

cannot

come

coming

could

D

do

down

F

for

friend

from

G

getting

goes

going

H

has

have

her

here

his

house

how

I

I

if

into

is

L

little

M

many

more

N

never

new

now

O

of

one

or

other

our

out

over

P

people

R

right

S

said

some

T

than

the

their

there

they

thing

to

tried

two

V

very

W

want

was

were

what

when

where

who

would

Y

you

your

Miss Jill's Ice Cream Shop

The Short *i* sound

in

it

him

Spelling Words

1. in
2. it
3. him
4. big
5. sit
6. did

Challenge Words

1. dish
2. milk

My Study List
Add your own
spelling words
on the back. ➡

Seasons

The Short *a* sound

an

at

can

Spelling Words

1. an
2. at
3. can
4. cat
5. had
6. man

Challenge Words

1. catch
2. add

My Study List
Add your own
spelling words
on the back. ➡

Take-Home Word List

Name _____

My Study List

_____

1. _____

2. _____

3. _____

4. _____

5. _____

6. _____

Take-Home Word List

Name _____

My Study List

_____

1. _____

2. _____

3. _____

4. _____

5. _____

6. _____

Go Away, Otto!

The Short *o* sound

on

not

box

Spelling Words

1. on
2. not
3. got
4. box
5. hot
6. top

Challenge Words

1. pond
2. doll

My Study List
Add your own spelling words on the back. ➡

At the Aquarium

Consonant Clusters with *r*

tr ip   cr ab

dr ip   gr in

Spelling Words

1. trip
2. crab
3. drip
4. grin
5. grab
6. trap

Challenge Words

1. crack
2. brown

My Study List
Add your own spelling words on the back. ➡

Name _____

My Study List

_____
- - - - - - - - - - - - - - - - -
1. _____

_____
- - - - - - - - - - - - - - - - -
2. _____

_____
- - - - - - - - - - - - - - - - -
3. _____

_____
- - - - - - - - - - - - - - - - -
4. _____

_____
- - - - - - - - - - - - - - - - -
5. _____

_____
- - - - - - - - - - - - - - - - -
6. _____

Name _____

My Study List

_____
- - - - - - - - - - - - - - - - -
1. _____

_____
- - - - - - - - - - - - - - - - -
2. _____

_____
- - - - - - - - - - - - - - - - -
3. _____

_____
- - - - - - - - - - - - - - - - -
4. _____

_____
- - - - - - - - - - - - - - - - -
5. _____

_____
- - - - - - - - - - - - - - - - -
6. _____

Challenge Words

1. add
2. dish
3. crack

Dog School

The Short *u* sound

up

us

but

Spelling Words

1. up
2. us
3. but
4. fun
5. cut
6. run

Challenge Words

1. jump
2. plum

My Study List
Add your own
spelling words
on the back. ➡

Two Best Friends

The Short *e* sound

get

ten

red

Spelling Words

1. get
2. ten
3. red
4. pet
5. men
6. yes

Challenge Words

1. tent
2. bell

My Study List
Add your own
spelling words
on the back. ➡

Name_____

My Study List

_____

_ _ _ _ _ _ _ _ _ _ _ _ _ _ _ _

1. _____

_____

_ _ _ _ _ _ _ _ _ _ _ _ _ _ _ _

2. _____

_____

_ _ _ _ _ _ _ _ _ _ _ _ _ _ _ _

3. _____

_____

_ _ _ _ _ _ _ _ _ _ _ _ _ _ _ _

4. _____

_____

_ _ _ _ _ _ _ _ _ _ _ _ _ _ _ _

5. _____

_____

_ _ _ _ _ _ _ _ _ _ _ _ _ _ _ _

6. _____

Name_____

My Study List

_____

_ _ _ _ _ _ _ _ _ _ _ _ _ _ _ _

1. _____

_____

_ _ _ _ _ _ _ _ _ _ _ _ _ _ _ _

2. _____

_____

_ _ _ _ _ _ _ _ _ _ _ _ _ _ _ _

3. _____

_____

_ _ _ _ _ _ _ _ _ _ _ _ _ _ _ _

4. _____

_____

_ _ _ _ _ _ _ _ _ _ _ _ _ _ _ _

5. _____

_____

_ _ _ _ _ _ _ _ _ _ _ _ _ _ _ _

6. _____

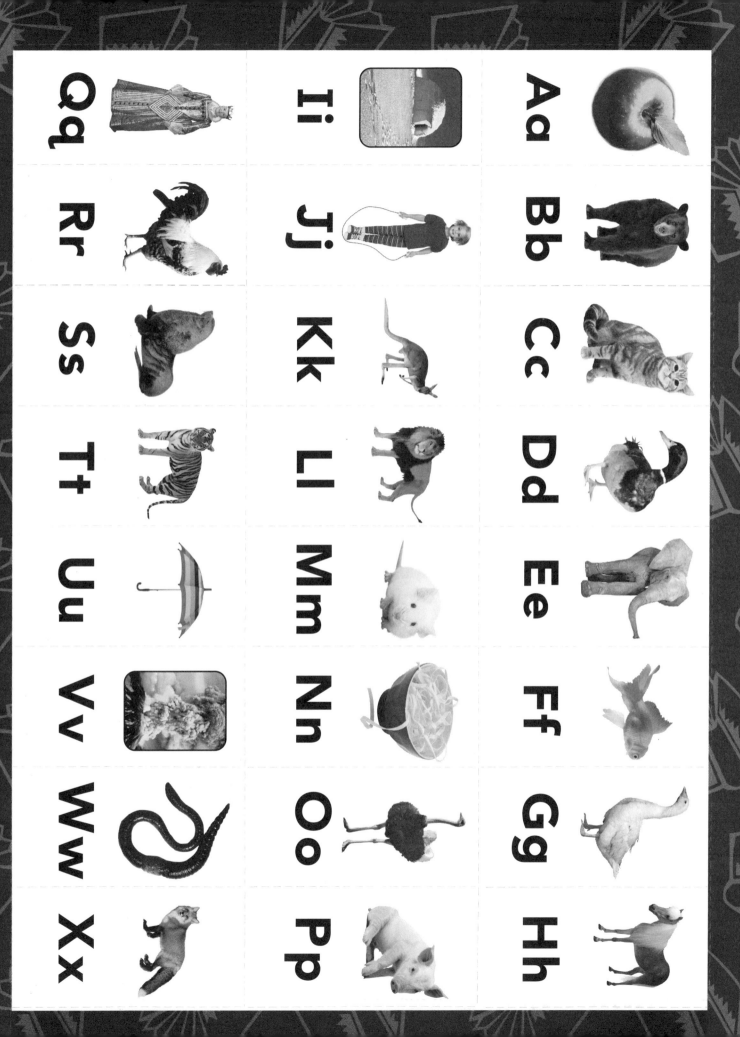

 a

 i

 qu_

 b

 j
ge
gi_
_dge

 r
wr_

 c
k
_ck

 k
c
_ck

 s
ce
ci_

 d
_ed

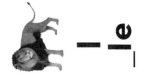 l
_le

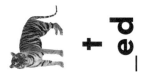 t
_ed

 e

 m

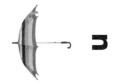 u

 f

 n
kn_
_gn

 v

 g

 o

 w

 h

 p

 _x

Yy

Zz

sh

th

wh

ch

a

i

o

u

e

oo

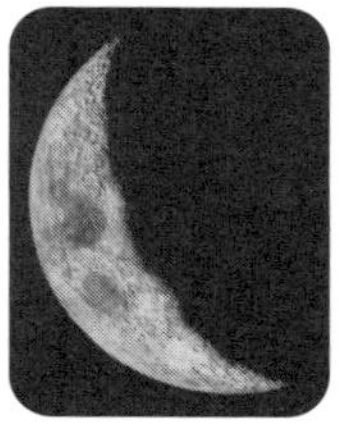

oo

ow

oy

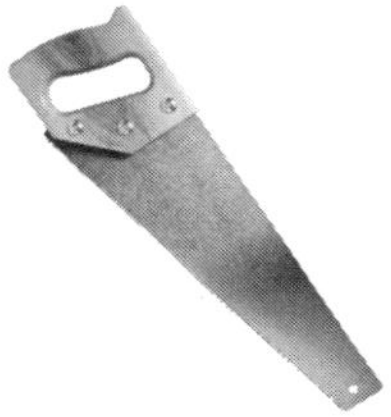

aw

or

ir

ar

y_

z
_s

sh

th

wh

ch
_tch

a
a_e
ai
_ay

i
i_e
ie
igh
_y

o
o_e
oa
ow
_oe

u
u_e
_ue
ew

e
e_e
ee
ea
_y
ie_

oo

oo
ew
ue
ou
u_e

ow
ou

_oy
oi

aw
au

or
ore

ir
er
ur

ar

Theme 1, Week 3	Theme 1, Week 2	Theme 1, Week 1
a	and	go
find	here	on
have	jump	the
one	not	
to	too	
who	we	

You can add your own words for sentence building.

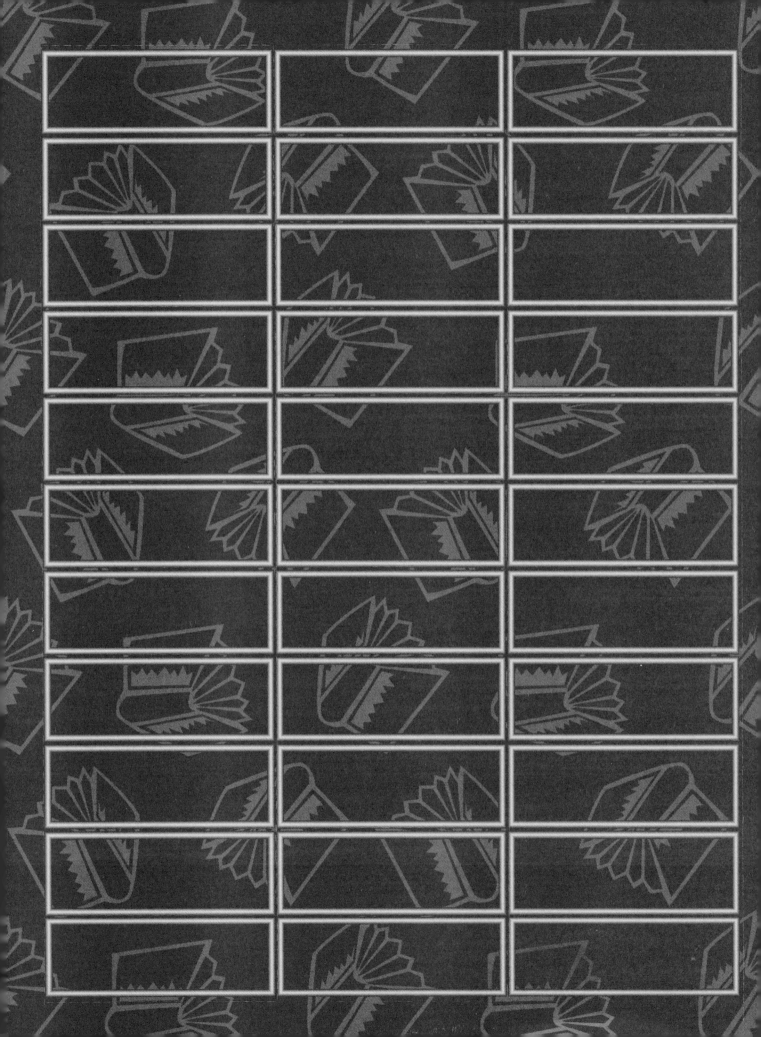

Theme 2, Week 3	Theme 2, Week 2	Theme 2, Week 1
are	do	five
away	for	four
does	is	in
he	me	once
live	my	three
pull	said	two
they	you	upon
where	I	what

You can add your own words for sentence building.

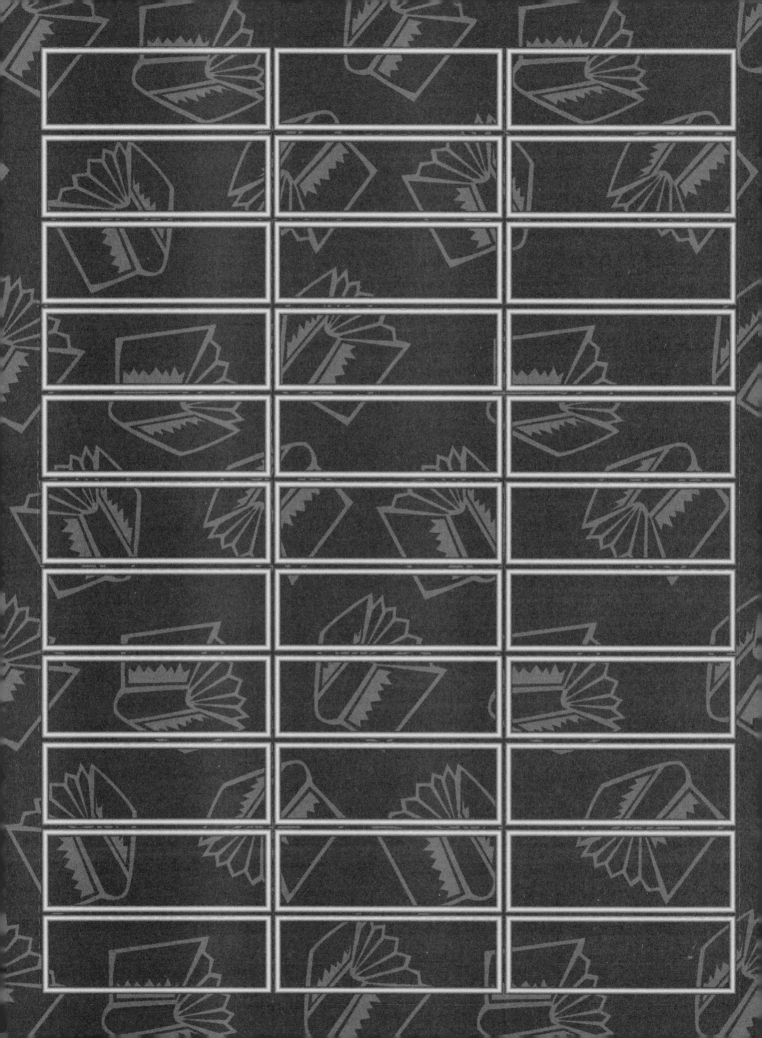

Theme 3, Week 3	Theme 3, Week 2	Theme 3, Week 1
also	all	animal
blue	call	bird
brown	eat	cold
color	every	fall
funny	first	flower
green	never	full
like	paper	look
many	shall	of
some	why	see

You can add your own words for sentence building.

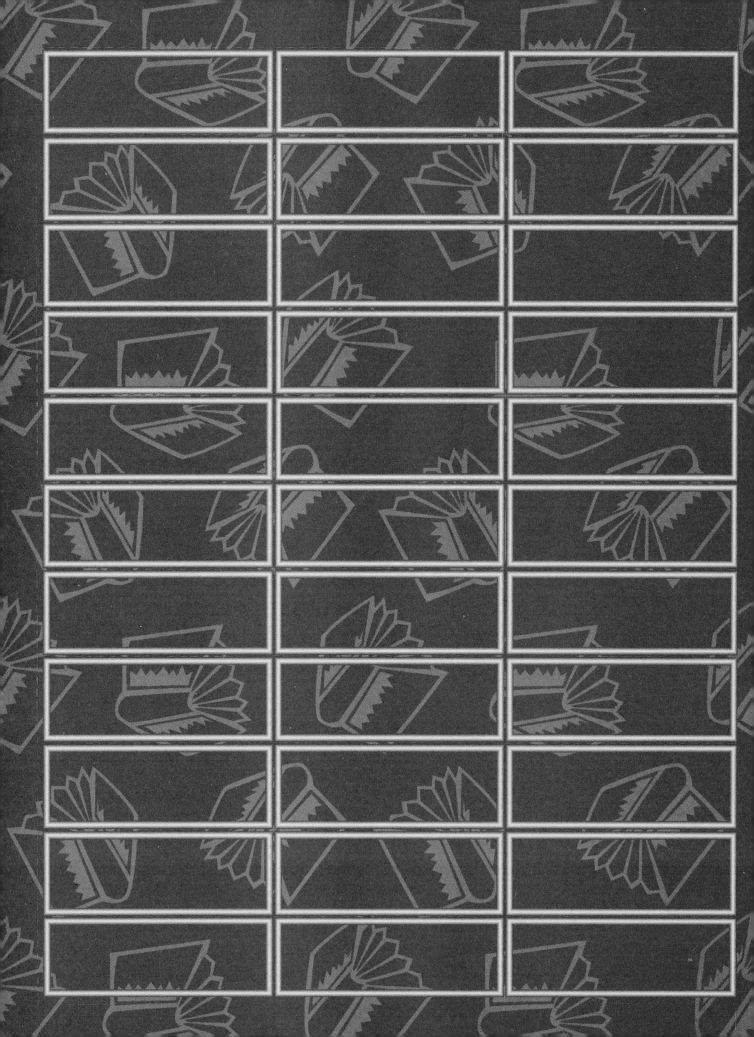

Theme 4, Week 3	Theme 4, Week 2	Theme 4, Week 1
car	play	come
down	friend	children
walk	girl	family
ear	she	father
hold	read	love
hur	sing	mother
learn	today	people
their	write	picture
would	know	your

You can add your own words for sentence building.

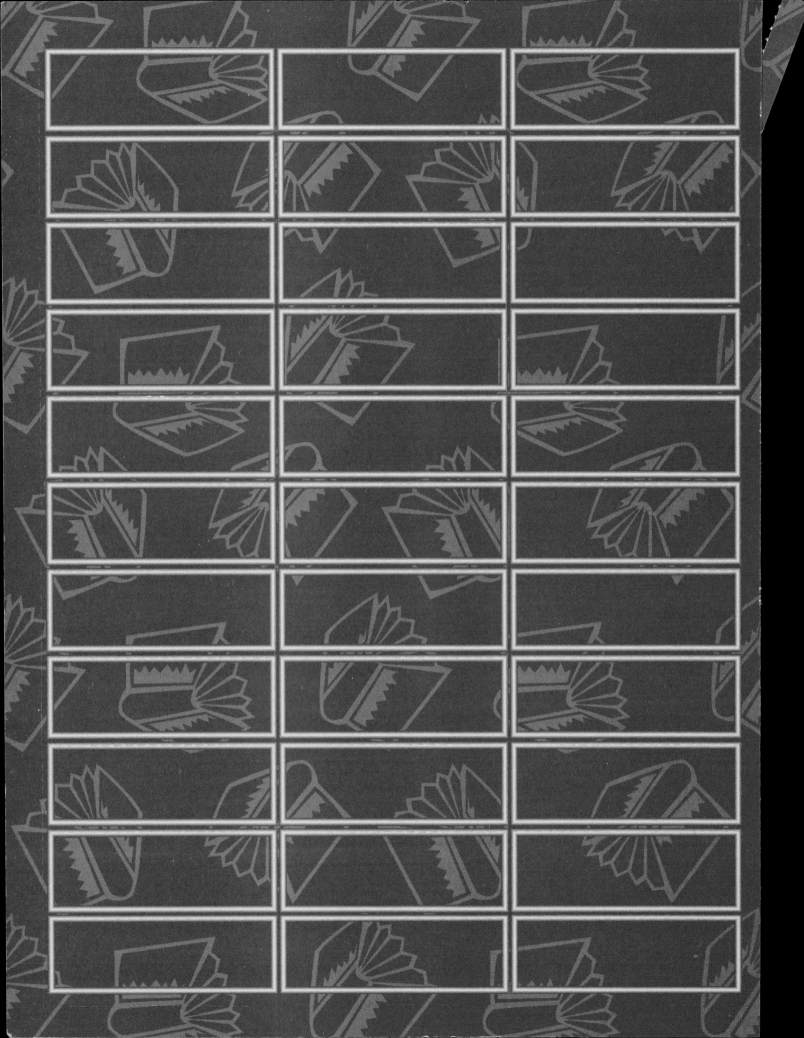